Detail from the Presence Chamber ceiling showing Apollo in his chariot.

CONTENTS

Kensington Palace from the south east by William Westall, 1819.

INTRODUCTION

Welcome to Kensington Palace, once a favoured home of some of Britain's most famous kings and queens and the setting for many great events and dramas in royal history.

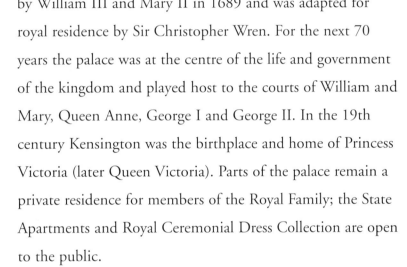

LEFT:
The ceiling of the King's Drawing Room by William Kent, 1722-3, showing Jupiter and Semele.

Kensington Palace from the south west by John Buckler, 1826. By this date the palace had long ceased to be the residence of the reigning monarch and was used to provide accommodation for other members of the Royal Family. A notable resident at this time was Princess Victoria (later Queen Victoria) who was born in the palace in 1819.

Originally a private country house, the building was acquired by William III and Mary II in 1689 and was adapted for royal residence by Sir Christopher Wren. For the next 70 years the palace was at the centre of the life and government of the kingdom and played host to the courts of William and Mary, Queen Anne, George I and George II. In the 19th century Kensington was the birthplace and home of Princess Victoria (later Queen Victoria). Parts of the palace remain a private residence for members of the Royal Family; the State Apartments and Royal Ceremonial Dress Collection are open to the public.

THE HISTORY OF KENSINGTON PALACE

William III (1689-1702) and Mary II (1689-1694)

When William III and Mary II came to the throne in 1689, the sovereign's principal London residence was Whitehall Palace. For purposes of state and ceremonial, it remained the official centre of the court in William III's reign, but neither he nor his wife Mary were attracted by the thought of living there. William suffered from chronic asthma and the damp riverside location of Whitehall threatened to weaken his already delicate health. Mary, for her part, felt shut-in there and, writing to her husband in 1690, complained: 'a poor body like me, who has been so long condemned to this place, and see nothing but water or wall'. Towards the end of February 1689 they moved out to Hampton Court, where extensive alterations were beginning under the direction of Sir Christopher Wren, Surveyor of the King's Works from 1669 to 1718. At the same time they began searching near London for a house which would be closer to Westminster and the business of government.

Mary II when Princess of Orange by William Wissing, 1685 (detail). The Queen took a keen personal interest in the building work at Kensington and visited the site often, eager to see the house completed.

In the summer of 1689 William and Mary purchased Nottingham House, a Jacobean mansion built about 1605 for Sir George Coppin, which stood in Kensington, a village that 'esteem'd a very good Air'. It was owned by William's trusted Secretary of State, Daniel Finch, Earl of Nottingham, and the purchase price was £20,000. According to the historian John Bowack, writing in 1705, it was 'the only retreat near *London*, he [William] was pleas'd with'.

Wren was instructed to improve the house immediately. Nicholas Hawksmoor was appointed Clerk of the Works (1689-1715) and the project was hurried forward, as the Queen was anxious to move in. In order to save time and money, the Jacobean house was left intact and Wren added blocks, or pavilions, to its four corners, to provide additional accommodation for the King and Queen and their court. Each pavilion was of three storeys, with attics above. Wren also reorientated the building by designing a new entrance and courtyard (the Great Court) on the west side (*see* 1689 plan, page 8).

Sir Christopher Wren, *Surveyor of the King's Works (1669-1718)* by Sir Godfrey Kneller, c1711.

LEFT:
William III when Prince of Orange by William Wissing, 1685 (detail). In 1689 William and Mary purchased Nottingham House for their winter residence. Writing in 1705, John Bowack noted how the King and Queen had 'spent the greater part of their leisure hours' there, being 'much pleas'd with its Airy Situation...[and] nearness to their Parliament'.

The south-east and north-west pavilions contained apartments for the King and Queen respectively, while the Council Chamber was situated in the north-east pavilion. The two lower floors of the Jacobean house were allocated to courtiers and the south-west pavilion contained the Great Stairs and the Chapel Royal. On the south side of the Great Court, Wren built a range containing a corridor (the Stone Gallery) which led from the main entrance to the south-west pavilion, with rooms for courtiers behind. On the north side of the courtyard were the kitchens and on the west, an

John Hayward's contract for carpenters' work on the new buildings at Kensington. The work to alter Nottingham House for the King and Queen began immediately and on 3 July 1689 contracts were signed with Thomas Hughes, bricklayer, and John Hayward, carpenter.

BELOW LEFT:
A modern reconstruction by Patrick Faulkner showing the south side of Nottingham House before it was transformed into a royal residence for William III and Mary II.

BELOW RIGHT:
Sutton Nicholls's engraving of the north side of Kensington House in 1689 showing two of the pavilions added by Wren to provide additional accommodation for the King and Queen.

archway surmounted by a clock tower, which still survives. Opposite the archway, on the far side of the present Palace Green, which was used as a parade ground, stood the barracks (later demolished); to the south of the green were the mews and stables, and to the west of these were the Surveyor's own house and the offices and yards of the Clerk of the Works.

A private road was also made through Hyde Park to Kensington, which was illuminated by a row of lamps. Beyond the road, Kensington Square was laid out with houses for court officials and within 15 years the village had grown to three times the size of Chelsea and, according to Bowack, was filled with 'Gentry and Persons of Note'.

While work on the building got underway, William and Mary took up temporary residence at Holland House nearby. Mary, however, felt unsettled there: 'I could not do as I would. This made me go often to Kinsington to hasten the workmen, and I was to impatient to be at that place, imagining to find more ease there...[but] part of the house which was new built fell down'. In spite of this disaster, which killed at least one workman and injured several others, the court took up residence at Kensington House shortly before Christmas 1689.

Although the court had moved in, the building was far from finished and in February 1690 the diarist John Evelyn called it 'yet a patch'd building'. In the summer of 1690, while William was away on campaign, Mary decided to launch a second round of improvements, which involved extending her apartments by the building of the Queen's Gallery, with its own staircase, and a separate block adjoining for her Maids of Honour (*see* 1690-1692 plan, page 8). This work was completed by the following spring. In November 1691, a fire that destroyed part of the southern range of the Great Court was made the occasion for a complete remodelling of the approach to the royal apartments: the King's Staircase was rebuilt in marble and a finely decorated Guard Chamber was constructed, facing the foot of the stairs.

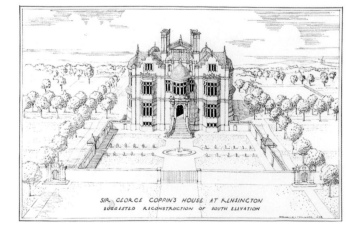

SIR GEORGE COPPIN'S HOUSE AT KENSINGTON
SUGGESTED RECONSTRUCTION OF SOUTH ELEVATION

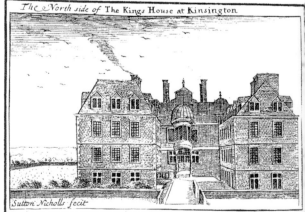

The North side of The Kings House at Kinsington

Sutton Nicholls fecit

Kensington was intended as a private retreat and the essentially domestic character of the building was underlined by the fact that it was never described as a palace, it was always referred to as Kensington House. It was principally a winter residence: at this time government business was conducted during the winter months and William spent his summers either abroad on campaign or visiting his native Holland. During his absences, Mary generally stayed at Whitehall, making occasional visits to Kensington.

During the late 17th and early 18th century, the court comprised well over 600 people who were living, working and often sleeping at Kensington Palace when the monarch was in residence. William and Mary's large-scale extensions to the property in 1689 were intended to provide adequate accommodation not only for themselves but also for this large household. Most of William's senior courtiers and household officers were allocated rooms in the palace, including his closest companions, the Earl of Portland and the Earl of Albemarle, who were granted spacious apartments near the King's own rooms.

In the early hours of Friday 28 December 1694 Mary died at Kensington of smallpox, at the age of 32. In the years that followed, much of her furniture was removed from the house, which was refurnished in grander style, and in 1699 the Queen's vast collection of oriental porcelain was given to the Earl of Albemarle. An inventory of 1697 listed nearly 800 items of porcelain in the palace, including many pieces of blue and white, now traditionally associated with Mary.

The last addition to the palace in William's time was the South Front, built in 1695, probably by Hawksmoor (*see* 1695 plan, page 8). The main feature of the new building was a long gallery at first floor level, the King's Gallery, in which William hung many works from his picture collection. William was a considerable connoisseur of painting and though he added little to the contents of the Royal Collection, he paid close attention to its maintenance and arrangement, and had the best pictures around him at Kensington. In April 1696, Evelyn wrote of 'Gallerys furnished with all the best pictures of all the [royal] houses, of Titian, Raphel, Corregio, Holben, Julio Romano, Bassan, V: Dyck, Tintoret & others'.

On a visit to Hampton Court in February 1702, William fell from his horse while riding in the park. Despite a broken collarbone, the King insisted on returning to Kensington almost immediately. He lay ill at the palace from 22 February until his death at 8.00am on Sunday 8 March.

Plans showing the development of Kensington Palace from 1689 to 1727

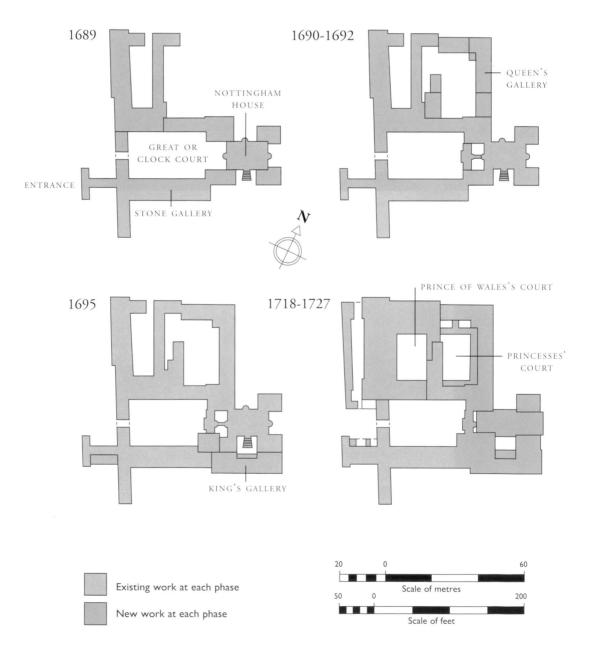

1689

NOTTINGHAM HOUSE

GREAT OR CLOCK COURT

ENTRANCE

STONE GALLERY

1690-1692

QUEEN'S GALLERY

N

1695

1718-1727

PRINCE OF WALES'S COURT

PRINCESSES' COURT

KING'S GALLERY

Existing work at each phase

New work at each phase

20   0   60
Scale of metres

50   0   200
Scale of feet

8

Queen Anne (1702-1714)

When Queen Anne, who had been living at nearby Campden House, succeeded to the throne in 1702, she extended her apartments by the addition of several new rooms within the small internal courtyard between what had been the old central block of Nottingham House and the King's Gallery. These were under construction in 1706. Apart from these modest alterations and other routine repairs, very few changes were made to the structure of the palace during her reign. However, the building was far from neglected and substantial quantities of new furniture were ordered for the Queen's apartments and for those of her consort, Prince George of Denmark. Many visitors to Kensington during this period commented upon the quality of the furniture and paintings, including Zacharius Conrad von Uffenbach who toured the palace in October 1710 and found it 'not very large but new and regular, having many handsome and well-furnished rooms'.

Queen Anne by Sir Godfrey Kneller, c1702. In the first few years of her reign, the Queen spent some £26,000 on improving the gardens at Kensington.

RIGHT:
Prince George of Denmark by Michael Dahl, c1705 (detail). After the Prince's death at Kensington on 28 October 1708, his body remained in the palace until 14 November when it was removed for burial in Westminster Abbey.

At Kensington Queen Anne is best remembered for her alterations to the gardens (*see* page 36). During her reign a number of outbuildings were constructed in the palace grounds, some of which still survive. Her principal memorial is the Orangery, built in 1704-5 to the north of the palace (*see* page 39).

Anne spent many long, contented hours at Kensington in the company of her intimate friend Sarah, Duchess of Marlborough, who was granted a large apartment in the palace and appointed Mistress of the Robes and Keeper of the Privy Purse shortly after Anne's accession. However, their friendship came to a bitter end after a quarrel at Kensington in 1710 and they never met again.

Both Anne and her husband died at Kensington. Anne was devastated by Prince George's death in October 1708, and did not stay at the palace again for almost 18 months. Six years later, just after dawn on 1 August 1714, the Queen died at the age of 49. Soon after her death, mourning was set up at the palace. The State Apartments were hung with black cloth and the Great Bedchamber was decked in purple, with a state canopy of the same material for the Queen's body to lie under.

George I (1714-1727)

The accession of George I was celebrated at Kensington with a bonfire in the gardens, where the household servants and courtiers toasted their new King with six barrels of strong beer and over 300 bottles of claret. This became a regular event and during the King's reign celebratory bonfires were held each year on 1 August - the anniversary of his accession.

The King's first visit to Kensington took place shortly after his arrival in Britain, when he inspected the palace and gardens and declared himself satisfied with both. However, a survey of 1716 found the building in a very poor state of repair and several designs for alterations were in the King's hands by April 1718. A plan for a dramatic rebuilding, to rival Blenheim Palace, was prepared by Sir John Vanbrugh, possibly as early as 1714. But such a transformation was not to be and the King chose a more modest proposal. The work was carried out under the supervision of William Benson, who had worked for the King in Hanover before he came to the throne, and who replaced Wren as Surveyor in 1718.

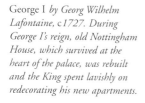

George I by Georg Wilhelm Lafontaine, c1727. During George I's reign, old Nottingham House, which survived at the heart of the palace, was rebuilt and the King spent lavishly on redecorating his new apartments.

The core of old Nottingham House, which survived at the heart of the palace, was replaced in 1718-22 by three new state rooms (the Privy Chamber, Cupola Room and Withdrawing Room) probably designed by Colen Campbell, the Deputy Surveyor, rather than by Benson (*see* 1718-1727 plan, page 8). The most striking feature of these rooms was the elaborate decorative painting of their ceilings. By rights this work should have been given to Sir James Thornhill, the Serjeant (or official royal) Painter, who was approached and asked to prepare designs and a quotation for decorating the first of the new apartments, the Cupola Room. However, his £800 fee was thought too costly and the little-known William Kent offered to paint the room in a similar design for £350. Kent won the commission and started work in the Cupola Room in 1722. His skill as a painter, strongly criticised by some, was evidently admired by George I, since between 1722 and 1727 he executed ceilings for nearly all the royal apartments at Kensington, and finished by decorating the King's Grand Staircase.

William Kent by Bartholomew Dandridge, c1730. Between 1722 and 1727, Kent was employed decorating the ceilings of nearly all the rooms in the royal apartments at Kensington. His self-portrait can be seen on the ceiling of the King's Grand Staircase.

Between 1724 and 1726 alterations were made to the two service courts on the north side of the palace. The western or Kitchen Court was entirely rebuilt and new kitchens were installed on the south side with a range of sculleries beyond. The north side was filled by a self-contained house, finely decorated in the Kent style, which may have been given to the Duchess of Kendal, George I's mistress. After the King's death in 1727, this house seems likely to have become the residence of his grandson, Frederick, Prince of Wales (the courtyard then receiving its present name, Prince of Wales's Court). At the same time an arcade was constructed round three sides of the eastern court which became known as Princesses' Court because the King's granddaughters lived there with their governess, the Dowager Countess of Portland (*see* 1718-1727 plan, page 8).

The extensive rebuilding work that George I initiated meant that he was able to make only limited use of the palace for much of his reign. In November 1723, Vanbrugh remarked that the court had been at Kensington 'so little for want of the New Rooms being ready for the King's use'. Furthermore, George I disliked the show and formality of court life and preferred to spend his time in his private apartments. The State Apartments were used only on public days, when the King was required to receive official visitors at the palace or when he formally entertained court society in the King's Drawing Room.

George II (1727-1760)

George II made Kensington one of his principal residences, usually spending between four and six months of the year there. However, during his long reign very few structural alterations were made to the palace and the only new building to be erected was a stable block built in 1740 for his younger son, William, Duke of Cumberland, who lived in a house (now destroyed) which stood to the north of Princesses' Court.

RIGHT:
George II by Enoch Seeman, c1730 (detail). George II was the last reigning monarch to live at Kensington Palace.

William Augustus, Duke of Cumberland by Charles Jervas, c1728. George II's five children all lived at Kensington Palace at various times. The Duke of Cumberland was allocated lodgings in a detached house to the north of the palace built by William III for the Earl of Albemarle.

After the death of his wife, Queen Caroline, in 1737, large parts of the palace fell into disuse, leading Horace Walpole to comment in 1749 that 'though there are so many vacant chambers [at Kensington], the King hoards all he can, and has locked up half the palace since the Queen's death'.

During the reigns of George I and George II, Kensington housed many of the finest paintings in the Royal Collection - 'much the best...of any of the royal palaces' one visitor wrote in 1738. In addition, many of London's leading furniture makers supplied the palace and thousands of pounds were spent furnishing the apartments in the latest fashion. The cabinet-makers, John Gumley and James Moore, for example, provided chandeliers, ornate mirrors, tables and stands for the three new state rooms in 1723-4 at a cost of over £1,700. The architecture of the building itself, however, was often considered modest in appearance and a guidebook of 1761 remarked that 'the palace indeed has none of that grandeur which ought to appear in the residence of a British monarch'.

The sudden death of George II at Kensington on 25 October 1760 ended an era in the history of the palace: it would never again serve as the seat of a reigning monarch.

An engraving after John Rocque (1736) showing Kensington Palace from the east during the reign of George II. The palace gardens were transformed during this period - note the newly planted avenues of trees and the Round Pond, completed in 1728 and still a focal point of the present Kensington Gardens.

When George III came to the throne in 1760 he showed little interest in Kensington, other than as a source for paintings, and preferred to live at Buckingham Palace. Throughout his long reign he rarely visited the palace and the building became 'utterly forsaken'. With no court life and no role for the State Apartments the palace soon fell into a state of disrepair.

Few alterations were made until the end of the 18th century, when apartments were required for some of George III's children and other members of the Royal Family. Over the next few years, vast sums were spent on accommodating them, causing the Duke of Wellington to remark that they were 'the damnedest millstone about the necks of any government that can be imagined'.

The Duke of Kent

In 1798 George III's fourth son, Edward, Duke of Kent (1767-1820), was allocated two floors of rooms in the south-east corner of the palace, beneath the State Apartments. These rooms had formerly been the king's private

apartments and seem to have been uninhabited since the death of George II in 1760, and were, therefore, in a fairly dilapidated state.

The poor condition of the building and the persistence of the Duke resulted in a complete conversion of the lower floors of the palace, the substance of which still survives. The architect was James Wyatt, Surveyor-General to the Board of Works from 1796 to 1813. A new porch was constructed on the eastern side of the Great Court, with an entrance hall which opened into a fine double staircase; this led to a saloon (the Red Saloon), with the dining room and others beyond. The work was finished by 1812 but four years later the Duke, having incurred huge debts, was forced to leave the country and live in Brussels.

Edward, Duke of Kent, by George Dawe, 1818 (detail). The Duke of Kent spent large sums on furnishing his apartments in the latest style. Between 1807 and 1811 he spent in excess of £19,000, in comparison to his brother, the Duke of Sussex, who had spent a mere £5,301 in the same period.

The unexpected death of the Prince Regent's daughter, Princess Charlotte, in 1817 altered his future plans. There was now no young heir to the throne and although George III had 12 living descendants, not one had a legitimate child. In 1818 the Duke married Victoria, Dowager Princess of Leiningen (1786-1861), the sister of Prince Leopold of Saxe-Coburg - the late Princess Charlotte's husband. He returned to England when his wife was expecting their first child and on 24 May 1819 Princess Victoria was born at Kensington Palace, in the ground-floor room in the north-eastern corner of his apartments. The young Princess was christened the following month in a private ceremony in the Cupola Room.

After the Duke's return to England he was allocated some of the rooms that had formerly been occupied by Caroline of Brunswick, Princess of Wales, to provide additional accommodation for his new family. Unfortunately, he lived only nine months after the birth of his daughter and died on 23 January 1820, only a few days before the death of his father, George III.

The Duchess of Kent and Princess Victoria

After the death of her husband, the Duchess of Kent and her daughter continued to live at Kensington until the accession of Queen Victoria in 1837. In the early part of William IV's reign (1830-37), the Duchess of Kent, noting how unused the State Apartments were, took the opportunity to extend her apartments on to the second floor. In 1832, Sir Jeffry Wyatville prepared a plan for her to partition the King's Gallery into three rooms, for Princess Victoria to use. The rooms adjoining the gallery to the south east were also converted into a bedroom, dressing room and maid's room. This by no means met with royal approval but was carried out none the less. When William IV visited the palace in 1836 and discovered that the Duchess and her daughter had taken over a suite of 17 rooms for their own use, he complained publicly that this had been done 'not only without his consent, but contrary to his commands'. It was in these newly acquired apartments, a year later, that Princess Victoria was awakened early in the morning of 20 June 1837 with news of her accession to the throne. The young Queen at once moved into Buckingham Palace, accompanied by her mother.

RIGHT:
Victoria, Duchess of Kent with Princess Victoria *by Henry Bone after Sir William Beechey (1821). The Princess is shown holding a miniature of her father, the Duke of Kent, who died when she was just a few months old.*

BELOW:
The Duke of Sussex in his library in the long first-floor room over the Stone Gallery. From London Interiors, *1840.*

BELOW RIGHT:
Augustus Frederick, Duke of Sussex *by Edward Miles, c1792-3. The Duke's lying in state at Kensington Palace in April 1843 drew vast crowds; it was estimated that some 15,000-20,000 people arrived to pay their respects.*

The Duke of Sussex

In 1805 the Duke of Kent's younger brother Augustus, Duke of Sussex (1773-1843), was allocated the former housekeeper's apartments in the south-west corner of the palace. Like William III, the Duke suffered badly from asthma and he became something of a recluse, devoting his energies to building up his extensive library. By the end of his life his collection filled ten rooms and comprised over 50,000 volumes.

The Duke was the most popular of the sons of George III and his death at Kensington Palace in April 1843 was the occasion of a genuine display of public mourning. His body lay in state in the palace and for one day the public were allowed to pay their last respects. A temporary wooden staircase was erected from a first-floor window to ease the flow of mourners. After his death, the Duke's wife, the Duchess of Inverness, continued to live in their apartments until 1873.

Caroline of Brunswick, Princess of Wales

Caroline of Brunswick, Princess of Wales by Sir Thomas Lawrence, 1804 (detail).

In 1804 Princess Caroline of Brunswick (1768-1821), the estranged wife of the Prince of Wales (the future King George IV), and their daughter Princess Charlotte (1796-1817), were allocated adjoining apartments in the north-east corner of the palace. However, the apartments were in need of repair and it was not until 1808 that they were ready for occupation.

Caroline had 11 rooms for her own use, all of which were splendidly furnished in the latest fashion. An additional 7 rooms were allocated to her ladies-in-waiting and a further 30 rooms for her staff. Until 1814, when she left England, the Princess divided her time between Kensington and her other home in Blackheath.

It is not certain whether Princess Charlotte ever made use of her apartments at Kensington, although she certainly visited her mother there. In 1808 her Lady-Companion wrote: 'She was at that time allowed to dine once a fortnight with the Princess of Wales, her Mother, at Kensington Palace.'

Princess Louise

Princess Louise, from a photograph of 1871.

Queen Victoria's sixth child, Princess Louise (1848-1939), and her husband, the Marquis of Lorne, occupied the Duke of Sussex's apartments after the death of his widow in 1873. Queen Victoria was delighted that one of her children should be living in her old home and wrote to her daughter after a visit: 'I can't tell you the feeling it gave me to see my old <u>Bedroom</u> and the old <u>doors</u> - and the <u>very view</u> I knew so well - and then downstairs to the old rooms where so <u>many</u> lived - including dear Papa!'

Princess Louise was one of the few women sculptors of the 19th century and by the age of 20 she had exhibited at the Royal Academy. Almost immediately after her arrival at Kensington she built her own studio, one of three that she was to use there over the years. Her most famous work, a marble statue of Queen Victoria at the time of her accession, stands outside the palace.

The Duke and Duchess of Teck

The Duke and Duchess of Teck with Princess Mary (later Queen Mary) in the garden of Kensington Palace, 1868.

In 1867 the Duke and Duchess of Teck were allocated the apartments formerly occupied by the Duke and Duchess of Kent and the young Princess Victoria. The Tecks had four children, all of whom were born at Kensington Palace. Their first, Victoria Mary, was born on 26 May 1867 and christened at the palace by the Archbishop of Canterbury. She later married the future King George V and as Queen Mary took a keen interest in the arrangement of the palace after it was opened to the public in 1899.

In 1883, the Tecks left Kensington to live in Florence and their apartments were later given to Princess Beatrice (1857-1944), the ninth and last child of Queen Victoria, who lived there from 1901 to 1940. The Royal Ceremonial Dress Collection is now housed in these rooms.

The State Apartments: 1837 to 1896

Although the private apartments at Kensington Palace continued to be used by members of the Royal Family throughout the 19th century, the State Apartments were sadly neglected and were used as stores for various paintings and furnishings from other palaces. By the end of the century the building was seriously dilapidated with the brickwork decaying and the woodwork infested with dry rot. In 1888, an article in *The Queen's Homes* described the State Apartments as 'empty - empty, bare, dreary, and comfortless; no carpets, no curtains, no furniture of any kind...nothing but bare walls and bare boards'.

Five years later, in 1893, an article in *The Graphic* exclaimed 'Surely something ought to be done to rescue this old palace from ruin?' Ideas for its future varied from demolition to use as a gallery or museum. It was only Queen Victoria's love for the palace in which she had grown up that saved it: in April 1897, Parliament was persuaded to pay for the restoration of the State Apartments on condition that they should be opened to the public.

The 1898 Restoration

ABOVE:
Queen Victoria *by Heinrich von Angeli, 1890. On 12 January 1898* The Times *reported the Queen's declaration that 'while she lived, the palace in which she was born should not be destroyed'.*

Queen Victoria arriving at Kensington Palace on 15 May 1899 to inspect the restoration of the State Apartments. This was the Queen's last visit to the palace.

The restoration of the State Apartments was carried out at great speed but with much care and attention to detail. According to Viscount Esher, the Secretary to the Office of Works, the aim was to restore the decoration 'as far as possible [to] exactly what it was in the reign of George II' using as little new work as possible.

In the King's Drawing Room, for example, the historian Ernest Law noted how William Kent's painted ceiling was 'so begrimed with the dirt, dust, smoke and smuts of upwards of a hundred and fifty years of London atmosphere, as to be nearly black'. It was cleaned 'with the most scrupulous care and practically no re-painting or re-gilding [was]...necessary'.

The State Apartments were opened to the public on Queen Victoria's 80th birthday, 24 May 1899. The newly restored rooms were hung with portraits and genre and history paintings illustrative of the periods and the monarchs associated with the palace. Queen Victoria took a keen interest in the pictures and exhibits, many of which concerned her reign and her image as Queen. For example, the three rooms in the south-east corner of the palace, where she and her mother had lived, were filled with portraits and objects relating to her life.

Early visitors to the palace looking at Princess Victoria's toys, including the doll's house she had left at Kensington when she became Queen.

The London Museum

In 1911-12 the State Apartments were given over to the newly founded London Museum for the display of royal relics and objects relating to the City of London. Queen Mary took a keen interest in the museum and it was she who managed to persuade George V that the museum could 'be accommodated, at least temporarily, in the State Rooms at Kensington Palace'.

The royal visit to the London Museum at Kensington Palace on 21 March 1912. George V, Queen Mary and two of their children are shown inspecting the exhibits in the Cupola Room.

The King and Queen toured the new museum on 21 March 1912, accompanied by Princess Mary and Prince George (later Duke of Kent). The State Apartments were filled with showcases, some containing hundreds of objects. In the Cupola Room, for example, there was a splendid display of London silver and several models of ships. There was also a large

collection of costume, including Georgian court dress (in the King's Gallery), coronation robes (in the Presence Chamber) and dresses worn by Queen Victoria, Queen Alexandra and Queen Mary.

The public were first admitted to the museum on 8 April 1912 and in the first day alone 13,000 visitors passed through the state rooms. However, Kensington had never been intended as a permanent home for the London Museum and in 1914 it moved to Lancaster House. After the museum left the State Apartments were closed and during the First World War (1914-18) they were used as offices by various charitable organisations. The palace did not reopen again until 1923, the hours then being restricted to Sunday afternoons only; from 1926 they were also open on Saturdays. In 1932-3 the three rooms associated with Queen Victoria were restored and rearranged under the direction of Queen Mary.

The Queen's Drawing Room as it appeared in 1912 shortly after the opening of the London Museum. This room was used to display porcelain, enamels and other items donated by Mr John Joicey, one of the museum's greatest benefactors.

Bomb damage during the Second World War (1939-45) left the State Apartments badly affected, particularly the Queen's Drawing Room and Dining Room, and by 1950 over £17,000 had been spent on their repair. After a five-year closure the palace was reopened on 4 June 1949. In the following year the London Museum returned to Kensington and for a quarter of a century (from 1950 until its amalgamation with the Guildhall Museum and its reopening in the Barbican as the Museum of London in 1976) occupied the lower floors originally converted for the Duke of Kent.

Kensington continues its long history as a residence for members of the Royal Family and there are still princesses living around Princesses' Court. The best known resident in recent years was Diana, Princess of Wales who occupied apartments in the north-west part of the palace from 1981 to 1997.

THE STATE APARTMENTS

When William III and Mary II extended Nottingham House in 1689, four new blocks, or pavilions, were added to the main house to provide additional accommodation for the King and Queen. The King's Apartments were in the south-east pavilion and the Queen's in the north-west. Despite later alterations, the basic layout of separate suites for the King and Queen survive. The extension of Nottingham House also included the creation of a new large courtyard and entrance on the west side. The visitor entrance is now through the Red Saloon on the queen's side of the palace.

Visitors should note that the selection of pictures on display in the State Apartments is changed from time to time.

The Garden Floor

ABOVE:
Detail from the ceiling of the King's Gallery showing Ulysses bound to the mast to listen to the Siren's song.

LEFT:
View looking from the Privy Chamber to the Cupola Room and the magnificent clock known as The Temple of the Four Grand Monarchies of the World.

The Garden Floor of Kensington Palace houses the Royal Ceremonial Dress Collection. The first two rooms, the Red Saloon and Teck Saloon, occupy part of the site of Nottingham House. Rebuilt for George I in the 1720s, these rooms were later remodelled by James Wyatt to provide accommodation for the Duke and Duchess of Kent and the young Princess Victoria. The apartment was later occupied by the Duke and Duchess of Teck. In more recent years, these rooms have been restored to reflect the style of decoration favoured by some of their 19th-century occupants.

Queen Victoria's first Privy Council was held in the Red Saloon on 20 June 1837, the day of her accession to the throne. The Duke of Wellington, who was present, wrote: 'she looked remarkably well; and was as much at her ease had as much self-possession; and was as gracious in her manner; as if she had been performing the part for years'.

The First Council of Queen Victoria *by Sir David Wilkie, 1838. This event took place in the Red Saloon on the day of the Queen's accession to the throne. The Queen in fact wore a black mourning dress but was depicted by the artist in white so that she stood out against the black coats of the councillors.*

18th-century Dress Rooms

The first dress room was originally William III's Little Bedchamber and later became Queen Caroline's Picture Closet. It is now used to display examples of dress worn at court between 1750 and 1770.

Silk brocade court mantua, c1750-3. This magnificent dress was probably worn at court by a member of the Flaxman or Spurrell family, both of whom lived near Norwich in Norfolk.

BELOW:
Detail of the embroidery on the back of a gentleman's court coat, c1800. In the later 18th century, gentlemen's court dress became flamboyant and costly. Fine lace, for example, was popular but very expensive and was often unpicked from one outfit so that it could be worn on another.

The mantua, worn by the lady, was a fashionable style of dress in the late 17th century and by the early 18th century had become the accepted dress worn by ladies on formal court occasions.

The lady is accompanied by a gentleman wearing a court suit dating from about 1770. His accessories include a 'chapeau bras', a hat made flat so that it could be carried neatly under the arm and not worn on the head.

The pink satin suit in the second room dates from about 1780 and is decorated with a style of embroidery in fine chain stitch, which was known as Beauvais work. The gentleman wears a court sword, the hilt decorated with cut steel. In his hand he carries a fob watch.

The rich velvet suit at the far end of the room dates from about 1790 and shows how, towards the end of the 18th century, the line of gentlemen's coats had become slimmer and the collars very high. The suit is embellished with very elaborate embroidery.

The display case near the fireplace shows how many components went together to create the 18th-century gentleman's court dress. Dressing for such occasions was a time-consuming business, and very often a manservant or valet would be called upon to assist.

The Passage Room

This room is hung with a collection of 18th-century prints, which include portraits of members of the Royal Family who used the palace during this period, as well as courtiers and court commentators. Also shown are royal ceremonies, examples of court dress and caricatures of some of the more extreme fashions of the day.

Leaving the Passage Room, the route passes briefly through the King's Gallery (which is revisited later in the tour) and on to the King's Grand Staircase.

The King's Grand Staircase

The King's Grand Staircase was originally built by Sir Christopher Wren in 1689 in a similar style to the Queen's Staircase. It was made of oak, and had plain panelled walls. When a new Guard Chamber (no longer surviving) was built at the foot of the stairs in 1692-3 the staircase was remodelled in marble, in a grander style.

The King's Grand Staircase. The fine wrought-iron balustrade, designed by the French ironsmith Jean Tijou, was added to the staircase when it was remodelled in the late 17th century.

Extensive alterations to the staircase were carried out for George I in the early 18th century. The panelling (with the exception of the dado) was removed, the windows were altered, a grand arcaded entrance was built at the foot of the stairs and, above this, both the top landing and the balustrade were extended to the west wall. Finally, the walls and ceiling were painted in a novel, continental manner by William Kent in 1725-7, for which he received £500.

The lower part of the walls is decorated simply with trophies, masks and sea horses picked out in gold against a stone-coloured background, while the upper part is treated more elaborately in the manner of Italian 16th-century illusionist painting. The perspective was designed to appear correct to a visitor as he mounted the staircase, which was the original approach to the King's Apartments.

The King's Grand Staircase by Charles Wild, published 1819. The 18th-century writer Horace Walpole was very critical of William Kent's work and grudgingly described the staircase as 'the least defective work of his pencil'.

On the upper part of the north wall (facing the landing), and part of the east, Kent painted an arcaded gallery crowded with members of George I's court. Among the group on the left are the Yeomen of the Guard and, standing nonchalantly outside the balustrade, a youth who was page to Lady Suffolk, the mistress of the Prince of Wales (later George II). The group at the far end of the north wall includes an elegant youth in Polish dress named Ulric, who was page to George I, and the King's two Turkish Grooms of the Chamber, Mahomet and Mustapha.

The figures on the east wall include Peter 'the wild boy', who was found in the woods near Hanover walking on all fours and climbing trees like a monkey; he was presented to the King who brought him to England and exhibited him as a curiosity. The remaining part of the east wall and the whole of the south wall are decorated in grisaille to simulate sculpture in architectural niches flanked by trophies.

The ceiling is designed to give the impression of a dome with balustraded openings, from which more onlookers gaze down upon the staircase. The group on the south side is made up of musicians, while that on the north includes Kent himself with his mistress, Elizabeth Butler, and two of his assistants.

The Presence Chamber

The Presence Chamber was originally part of the south-west pavilion added to Nottingham House by Wren in 1689. It was used for formal receptions and it was here on 1 August 1734 that George II, seated on his throne and attended by various officers of state, received a party of Indian chiefs from the Cherokee tribe, 'their faces...variously painted after their Country ['s] manner, some half black, others triangular, and others with bearded Arrows instead of Whiskers'.

The ceiling of the Presence Chamber, painted by William Kent in 1724.

The room was altered for George I, and the doors, with their plainly moulded surrounds, were inserted at this time. The extraordinary ceiling, for which Kent was paid in 1724, was decorated in the 'grotesque' style derived from Italian 16th-century painting in the antique manner. The central roundel, supported by four bright-red diagonal bands, shows Apollo (the sun god) in his chariot. Kent's design, unlike anything seen in England since the days of Inigo Jones (1573-1652), was criticised by some, including the antiquarian scholar George Vertue (1683-1756) who called it 'poor stuff'. However, it was obviously appreciated by the King, for Kent decorated the ceilings of the Council Chamber and the King's Bedchamber (which no longer survive) in a similar style.

The Presence Chamber by James Stephanoff, published 1816. This water-colour shows the room densely hung with paintings which virtually obscure the tapestried walls beneath.

OPPOSITE:
The Privy Chamber (detail) by Charles Wild, published 1816.

The walls are hung with a set of rare 17th-century Italian embroideries depicting scenes from the New Testament. The panels are: *The Adoration of the Magi*, *The Rest on the Flight into Egypt* and *Penance* (or *Christ in the House of Simon the Pharisee*). In front of these are terracotta busts of George II and Queen Caroline by Michael Rysbrack, dated 1738 and 1739 respectively.

The overmantel, decorated with a composition of drapery, birds, fruit, flowers and cherubs' heads, was carved by Grinling Gibbons (1648-1721). This came originally from the King's Gallery and was moved to the King's Drawing Room in 1721 and then to here in 1724. The overmantel painting, *A Classical Landscape*, is by Hendrick Danckerts, signed and   dated 1677, and shows two women talking at the foot of a statue.

Detail of the overmantel in the Presence Chamber by Grinling Gibbons. Gibbons was made Master Carver to the Crown in 1693 and executed many fine carvings for William III.

A giltwood chair of state, similar to the one on display, would have originally sat in this room underneath a grand damask canopy.

The Privy Chamber

This room served as an audience chamber of a more intimate character than the Presence Chamber and to which fewer people were admitted. It is hung with three Mortlake tapestries, part of a set, probably woven for

Charles I when Prince of Wales, in 1623-4, representing the seasons of the year, and illustrating the months of February, July and August and November. The series of 18th-century busts below the tapestries represent distinguished early scientists and philosophers - Samuel Clarke, Sir Isaac Newton, John Locke, Robert Boyle and William Wollaston - and were made by Michael Rysbrack and Giovanni Battista Guelfi for the Hermitage in Richmond Gardens, built by Kent for Queen Caroline. The statue of a Moor in the centre of the room was executed by John van Nost the Elder, probably for William III. It has been at Kensington since at least 1710 when Zacharius Conrad von Uffenbach saw it in the King's Gallery: 'In one corner was the bust of a Moor very well done from life - made, indeed, of nothing but coloured stones, with great skill.' The 18th-century bust of the actor David Garrick, is by an unknown sculptor.

The magnificent ceiling was painted by Kent, who received £300 for his work in 1723. It is painted in imitation of a series of ceiling paintings in ancient Rome and shows Mars (wearing the Order of the Garter) and Minerva surrounded by the arts and sciences. The allusion to the King and Queen would have been obvious to members of the court.

RIGHT:
Detail of the Privy Chamber ceiling showing Mars and Minerva presiding over the arts and sciences.

24

The Cupola Room

The Cupola, or Cube, Room was the principal state room of the palace, and the most lavishly decorated. It was here that Kent began work in 1722. His intention was to conjure up an image of Roman grandeur, an embodiment of the virtues of the Hanoverian monarchy; the architectural setting, the painting and the statuary were all devised to this end.

The dominant architectural elements of the room are the giant Ionic pilasters and the massive grey marble doorways supported by Ionic columns. Kent made extensive use of *trompe l'oeil* and much of the architectural decoration is painted, including the fluting of the pilasters and the carving of the mouldings to the bases.

Above the fireplace is a bronze bust and an impressive bas-relief depicting a Roman marriage, commissioned from Michael Rysbrack in 1723-4.

The Cupola Room functioned as a reception and meeting room for the grandest and most formal gatherings. It was here that Princess Victoria was christened by the Archbishop of Canterbury in 1819.

The niches around the room contain gilded lead statues of Roman gods and goddesses, Bacchus, Ceres, Juno, Apollo, Diana and Mercury, and above these are plaster casts of a series of Roman emperors which replace lost originals.

The commission for the ceiling was the subject of a fierce argument between George I's Serjeant (principal) Painter, Sir James Thornhill, and the new royal protégé, William Kent (*see* page 10). The commission was finally given to Kent in 1722, who undercut his rival and promised to complete it for a total of £350, which included using the expensive blue pigment, ultramarine. The design, inspired by Thornhill's more distinguished, but rejected, scheme, is painted with octagonal coffers (ornamental sunken panels) in blue and gold, diminishing in size towards the top of the ceiling to give an optical illusion of height. In the centre is a large octagonal panel enclosing the Star of the Order of the Garter. The Board of Works showed little confidence in Kent's workmanship, for in May 1722 they invited a committee of three artists to inspect it. They reported: 'tis our opinion that the perspective is not just, that the principall of the worke...is not done as such a place requires...that the boys, masks, mouldings etc far from being well [they have] seen very few worse for such a place'. Doubt was also thrown on Kent's use of ultramarine, implying that he was cheating the Board. However, scientists have since been able to confirm his use of this pigment during recent conservation work.

Gilded statue of Mercury in the Cupola Room. The antiquarian scholar George Vertue (1683-1756) criticised the statues: 'guilt with burnish'd gold, which makes a terrible glaring show, & truly gothic'.

The four, twelve-branch chandeliers, suspended from the mouths of the painted heads on the ceiling, are reproductions of the lost originals made by the firm of Gumley and Moore in 1723-4. They also supplied furniture for

the room, including a set of fine marble-topped side tables supported on sphinxes; these have long since been removed.

The clock in the centre of the room was acquired by Augusta, Princess of Wales, the mother of George III. It was begun by Charles Clay and completed in 1743 by John Pyke; it once contained a musical box that played tunes by Handel, Corelli and Geminiani. The painted scenes on the sides by Jacopo Amigoni, illustrate the four great monarchies of antiquity mentioned in the book of Daniel: Chaldaea, Persia, Macedonia and Rome. The original plinth of the clock has been reproduced, after an engraving by Hubert-François Gravelot of c1743.

The King's Drawing Room

The Drawing Room was the focal point of court life where, on public days, the king would meet members of the court, dressed in their finery. The assembly became known as a 'Drawing Room', and these public days at court were frequently held on Thursdays and Sundays when the Royal Family also dined in public.

William Kent was responsible for the original furnishing and decoration of the room but, unfortunately, little of this survives, with the exception of the chimney-piece and the ceiling. The chimneypiece, carved in 1724 by James Richards, the King's Master Carver, was removed to St James's Palace in 1822-4 but restored to its original position in 1974. It originally had a great overmantel framing *The Holy Family with Saint Francis* by Peter Paul Rubens (1577-1640).

Soon after George I's death, the picture hang in the King's Drawing Room became a matter of dispute between George II and his wife, Queen Caroline. According to the diarist and courtier Lord Hervey, the Queen rearranged the picture hang in 1735 during the King's absence in Germany and he demanded that it be reinstated on his return, insisting 'I will have them taken away and the old ones restored.' One of the paintings which he insisted on returning was the *Venus and Cupid* by Giorgio Vasari (1511-74) after Michelangelo (which hangs on the south wall opposite the fireplace), and which the King referred to as his 'fat Venus'.

Kent's ceiling painting, for which a payment of £500 was made in May 1723, shows Jupiter appearing to his lover, Semele, who he inadvertently destroyed with his divine power. The central panel is surrounded by a deep oval frame in a simulated architectural setting.

Detail of the chimneypiece in the King's Drawing Room, carved in 1724 by James Richards to Kent's design.

Like the Cupola Room, the King's Drawing Room was lit by four carved, gilt chandeliers made by Gumley and Moore. They were originally suspended from the orbs in the corners of the ceiling, outside the oval frame. The Drawing Room furniture was also probably supplied by Gumley and Moore and included one armchair (for the king), twenty-four stools, two looking glasses, two tables and four carved, gilt stands. The room was hung with crimson damask which has been rewoven to a George I pattern.

With the exception of the Vasari, the paintings in this room are mainly 17th-century in date. Over the door from the Cupola Room is *St John the Baptist*, attributed to Jusepe de Ribera. The two paintings by Benedetto Gennari on the west wall, *Venus and Sleeping Adonis* and *The Triumph of Galatea*, are part of a set of four painted for Charles II in about 1676, that hung in his dining-room at Windsor. The overdoor portraits of Venetian Doges are by Odoardo Fialetti and were acquired by Sir Henry Wotton when he was ambassador in Venice and bequeathed by him to Charles I.

The Council Chamber

This room is used for temporary exhibitions and is not always open.

William III's original Council Chamber is housed in Wren's north-east pavilion. The room retained this function in the reigns of George I and George II but later fell into disrepair. It was remodelled in the early 19th century by James Wyatt. The cast-iron columns are a slightly later attempt to support the sagging floor. This room is now used for temporary displays relating to the history of the palace and its residents.

Miniature of Princess Victoria by Henry Collen, 1836. This portrait shows the young Princess at the age of 17, the year before she became Queen.

Queen Victoria's Bedroom

The next three rooms were originally part of the King's Apartments and were converted for the Duchess of Kent and Princess Victoria in 1834-6. In 1932-3, they were rearranged by Queen Mary to show how they might have appeared in Princess Victoria's time. They are furnished with many items that belonged to Queen Victoria and Prince Albert.

The room known as Queen Victoria's Bedroom was originally the King's State Bedchamber and its ceiling was decorated by Kent 'in grotesque painting' in 1723 (this no longer survives). It was here that Princess Victoria was awoken in the early hours of 20 June 1837 with the news of the death of her uncle, King William IV, and of her accession to the throne. Thirty years later, in 1867, the Duke and Duchess of Teck were allocated these apartments and their first child, Victoria Mary (the future Queen Mary, wife of George V) was born in this room.

Sir George Hayter's large painting of the marriage of Queen Victoria and Prince Albert at St James's Palace on 10 February 1840 hangs on the south wall. Queen Victoria and Prince Albert delighted in giving each other paintings for their birthdays or at Christmas and between them they acquired or commissioned many pictures, some of which are displayed in these rooms. The painting over the mantelpiece is *L'Amante* by Augustus Egg, purchased by Prince Albert in 1841; it is flanked by two paintings by William Edward Frost: *The Disarming of Cupid* and *Una among the Fauns and Wood-Nymphs*, which were given by Queen Victoria to the Prince Consort on his birthdays in 1849 and 1847 respectively.

Queen Victoria's Bedchamber is hung with paintings that belonged to the Queen and her consort, Prince Albert, many of which depict their children or members of their family. Above the bed hangs a portrait of their son, Albert Edward, Prince of Wales (later King Edward VII) by Wilhelm Hensel, dated 1843.

RIGHT:
Queen Mary by Sir Oswald Birley, 1934 (detail). Victoria Mary, Princess of Teck (later Queen Mary) was born in Queen Victoria's Bedroom in 1867. As Queen, she took a keen interest in Kensington Palace and in 1932-3 restored and rearranged the three rooms associated with Princess Victoria and the Duchess of Kent.

On the north wall, above the bed, are portraits of Queen Victoria's half-sister, Feodora, and her husband Ernest, Prince of Hohenlohe-Langenburg, both signed and dated 1839 by Carl Leybold. Feodora lived at Kensington for much of Victoria's childhood and the two princesses were inseparable.

To the right of the fireplace, on the writing table, is a portable writing desk used by Queen Victoria as a child; and in the corner is a bust of Prince Albert by Emil Wolff, signed and dated Rome, 1839. The bed, which belonged to Queen Victoria, was brought from Buckingham Palace by Queen Mary in 1932-3; the chaise-longue at its foot was the Duchess of Kent's favourite sofa, and the ornate gilt table beside the bed was made for Queen Victoria's first railway saloon.

Between the windows are a pair of walnut cabinets, given by the Duchess of Teck to her daughter Victoria Mary in about 1872 and placed in the Princess's schoolroom at Kensington Palace. The busts by Mary Thornycroft, dated 1846, are of Queen Victoria's eldest children, the Princess Royal and the Prince of Wales (the future King Edward VII).

Ante Room

This room was originally part of the King's Great Closet and the door in the west wall led to the King's back-stairs. The chintz curtains and pelmets, patterned with roses, reproduce those introduced by Queen Mary in 1932-3.

The room is hung with paintings collected by Queen Victoria and Prince Albert, including, on the south wall, *The Victoria Cow* by Thomas Sidney Cooper. The cow was sent to the Queen from Jersey in 1843 and was said to have been named 'Victoria' from the 'V' shaped mark between its horns. The picture was commissioned by the Queen who was said to be delighted with the finished work.

The Duchess of Kent's Dressing Room

Victoria, Duchess of Kent
by Sir George Hayter, 1835
(detail). The Duchess presented
this painting to Princess Victoria
on her 15th birthday. It was
later hung in her study at
Kensington Palace.

RIGHT:
The Duchess of Kent's Dressing
Room. The double armchair in
the centre of the room originally
stood in Queen Victoria's sitting-
room at Buckingham Palace and
was brought to Kensington by
Queen Mary in 1932-3. The
late 17th-century giltwood cradle
is German and was acquired by
Queen Victoria in 1843.

The Duchess of Kent's Dressing Room was originally part of William III's private apartments, and there was formerly a wall across the centre of the room dividing it into the Great Closet and the Little Closet; the ceilings of which were among those painted by Kent for George I. The wallpaper and curtains reproduce those which existed when the room was occupied by the Duchess of Kent and Princess Victoria. The furniture, pictures and objects in this room, which is furnished as a sitting-room, date almost entirely from the 1840s and 1850s.

The pictures on the west wall (opposite the windows) include a portrait of the Duke of Sussex, Queen Victoria's uncle (who had an apartment in the south-west corner of the palace from 1805 to 1843), painted by James Lonsdale in c1823. The portrait of the Duchess of Kent with the young Princess Victoria, who is shown holding a miniature of her father, was painted in 1821 by Sir William Beechey, probably for the Princess's uncle, Prince Leopold. The Princess and her mother posed for the artist at Kensington Palace in May 1821, after having delayed the sitting due to Victoria suffering a 'slight cold'.

Over the door on the north wall hangs a portrait of Princess Victoria's father, the Duke of Kent by George Dawe, signed and dated 1818 and purchased by the Queen in 1839. Above the Erard piano, is John Martin's dramatic *Eve of the Deluge*, which was commissioned by Prince Albert and painted in 1840. A small bust of Queen Victoria's second son, Prince Alfred, by Mary Thornycroft, sits on the small round table in the centre of the room. In the corner of the room is another bust by Thornycroft, of the Duchess of Kent - both are signed and dated 1847.

The King's Gallery

Ceiling detail from the King's
Gallery showing Ulysses kneeling
at the feet of King Alcinous and
Queen Arete.

The King's Gallery was built for William III in 1695 and was originally furnished with green velvet hangings and white damask curtains. The room, which is 96ft long, was intended as a gallery for the finest pictures in the Royal Collection.

In November 1700 the *London Gazette* reported that the King had returned from Hampton Court to celebrate his birthday at Kensington where there were 'Entertainments for the Ladies, and other Persons of Quality in the Great Gallery'. It was also here in the gallery, on 3 March 1702, that William was taken ill, a few days after his riding accident at Hampton Court. The *Post Boy* recorded: '[On] Wednesday last...he took several Turns

in the Gallery at Kensington, but at length finding himself feeble and weary, he sat down, and fell a-sleep, which tis thought occasion'd him to take cold, for when he awak'd he had a Shivering Fit, which turn'd to a Fever.' The King died five days later, on 8 March 1702, aged 51.

The King's Gallery has been refurbished following the decorative scheme devised for George I. In 1725, the King commissioned William Kent to design and decorate a new gallery which had to incorporate the carved cornice and other decorative features designed for William III. The wind-dial above the chimneypiece, for example, was made for William by Robert Morden in 1694 but Kent was asked to design a new marble chimneypiece and carved overmantel around it. The points of the compass are marked round the circumference of a map of north-western Europe and the direction of the prevailing wind is indicated by the pointer operated by rods connected to a wind-vane on the roof. In the corners are painted scenes, probably by Robert Robinson, illustrating the four continents (Australia was not discovered until the later 18th century). Above the wind-dial, set in a circular frame is a small fresco of the Madonna and Child, which was traditionally ascribed to Raphael and is now thought to be the work of the 16th-century Italian artist Annibale Carracci.

Kent was also responsible for designing new doorcases for the gallery and inserting two false doors. The woodwork was painted and gilded, probably by Sir James Thornhill, and has been re-created together with the hand-woven 'rich crimson genoa damask' hangings and curtains trimmed with lace. The gallery was also furnished at this period with stools, elbow chairs, marble tables and stands, and lit by chandeliers and six silver sconces (lights) hanging between the windows. There were also a number of pieces of statuary, including *The Four Seasons* by Camillo Rusconi (1658-1728), copies of which are now displayed in the gallery. The originals remain at Windsor Castle.

In January 1725 Kent and an assistant began work on the ceiling, following approval by George I. The paintings, executed on canvas, depict scenes from the story of Ulysses. The seven mythological scenes were painted by Kent himself, but all the surrounding decorative work was done by his Spanish assistant, Francisco de Valentia (of whom nothing is known), whose name is inscribed on the back of one of the canvases.

The picture hang in the gallery was selected by Kent for George I and included two important masterpieces by Sir Anthony van Dyck (1599-1641): on the west wall *Charles I and Henrietta Maria with their Two Eldest Children* (called 'The Greate Peece') and on the east wall *Charles I with M de St Antoine* (his equerry). These two paintings now hang at Buckingham Palace but a 17th-century copy of *Charles I with M de St Antoine* can be seen in place of the original. The paintings on the north wall (opposite the windows) include two magnificent canvases by Jacopo Tintoretto (1518-94): *The Muses* and *Esther before Ahasuerus*. Both were recorded as hanging in the gallery during the reign of George II.

Charles I with M de St Antoine by Sir Anthony van Dyck, 1633. This painting was hung on the east wall of the gallery during the reign of George I. A later copy now hangs in place of the original.

In 1835 the gallery was partitioned into three rooms for the Duchess of Kent and Princess Victoria. The young Princess described the new rooms in her *Journal*: 'the old gallery...is portioned into three large, lofty, fine cheerful rooms. One only of these is ready furnished; it is my sitting-room and is *very* prettily furnished indeed...The next is my study, and the last is an ante-room'. Traces of the patterned red wallpaper used in the Princess's sitting-room were discovered when the King's Gallery was restored in 1993-4.

The route now takes the visitor back through the Presence Chamber and Privy Chamber to the queen's side of the palace.

Queen Mary's Drawing Room

Queen Mary's Drawing Room is the first of a series of small rooms which were used by the queen as her private apartments.

This room was badly damaged by incendiary bombs on the night of

14 October 1940; the panelling was destroyed and the walls are now covered with a modern paper. The cornice, which survived in part, is elaborately carved with acanthus leaves and the monogram of William and Mary surmounted by a crown. The giltwood chandelier, which is probably English, *c*1730, was one of four originally hung in the Queen's Gallery.

On the south wall is a late 17th-century inlaid cabinet, probably made by the royal cabinet-maker Gerrit Jensen for Kensington Palace, which contains 17th and 18th-century oriental porcelain. The portrait beside the cabinet is of George Byng, First Viscount Torrington, by Sir Godfrey Kneller (1646?-1723). The barometer in the corner is by Thomas Tompion and was also probably made for the palace in about 1695. On the north wall is a late 17th-century inlaid ebony writing table, typical of the style of furniture preferred by Queen Mary, above which hangs a fine pastoral landscape by the 17th-century Flemish artist David Teniers the Younger.

The portrait between the windows, from the studio of Kneller, shows George I in robes of state. Above the fireplace is a portrait by Johann Kerseboom of the scientist Robert Boyle (1627-91), a founder member of the Royal Society.

Queens Mary's Bedchamber

The bedchamber originally had a splendid marble chimneypiece decorated with William III's coat of arms and an overmantel carved by

Grinling Gibbons, but the fine cornice is the only decorative work that remains. The windows in this room were originally in the south wall (opposite the bed) but were blocked when old Nottingham House, at the heart of the palace, was rebuilt in 1718-22, and the windows in the west wall were opened as replacements. The wide elm floorboards in the room are the only original boards to survive in any of the State Apartments.

The state bed is sometimes known as the 'warming-pan bed' and is traditionally associated with the birth of Prince James Francis Edward Stuart (the 'Old Pretender') at St James's Palace in 1688. The young Prince, son of James II and Mary of Modena, was the Catholic heir to the throne and news of his birth was not well received by the Protestant supporters of William of Orange (the future William III). Within hours a rumour was circulating that the infant was not the Queen's child, but a surrogate baby smuggled into the bed in a warming pan. In recent years the bed has been thoroughly examined and it appears to have been made up from several beds of various periods, although it is likely that some of the principal hangings were made for James II and his consort, whose crowns and cyphers appear on the headcloth and board.

The large marquetry cabinet dates partly from the mid-17th century and is probably French. It is inlaid with semi-precious stones and was purchased by George IV. It is similar in style to one that belonged to Queen Mary, which formed part of the original furnishings of this room. The inlaid mirror and table between the windows date from the late 17th century.

Queen Mary's Bedchamber. Queen Mary II died at Kensington in 1694, probably in this room. After her death, the palace, including the Privy Chamber, Presence Chamber and the King's own bedchamber, was decked out in black and purple mourning cloth.

LEFT:
Queen Mary's Drawing Room by James Stephanoff, published 1817. In the early 19th century this room was known as the Admiral's Gallery after the portraits of admirals that were hung here.

Queen Mary's Dining Room

Queen Mary's Dining Room. Household records show that William and Mary had an extremely generous daily allowance of food and drink, although simple suppers of fish and beer were not uncommon. This room still retains its original marble fireplace and panelling, although it may have once been hung with gilt leather and tapestries.

Queen Mary's Dining Room was originally a square room but was reduced in size in the 19th century by the creation of a passage along its rear (west) wall, so that the coving now comes to an abrupt end. The recess, which was once a small closet, now houses a late 17th-century black lacquer cabinet on which is displayed 17th and 18th-century Chinese porcelain of the type avidly collected by Queen Mary. The inlaid gate-leg table and high-backed armchairs also date from the late 17th century.

The portrait over the fireplace is of Katherine Elliot, nurse to the infant James II and later Dresser and Woman of the Bedchamber to both his wives. It was painted by John Riley and Johann Baptist Closterman around 1687-8.

Queen Mary's Closet

Sarah Churchill, Duchess of Marlborough, after Sir Godfrey Kneller, c1700 (detail). The Duchess was Queen Anne's closest friend and the two corresponded incessantly, using the invented names of Mrs Morley (the Queen) and Mrs Freeman (the Duchess) to demonstrate the equality of their relationship.

This small closet was the scene of Queen Anne's last meeting with Sarah, Duchess of Marlborough, which took place on the evening of Maundy Thursday, 6 April 1710. The Duchess was Anne's great favourite and held several important positions in the Queen's household, including First Lady of the Bedchamber. However, their friendship ended after a disagreement, which was never resolved, and in 1711 the Duchess resigned all her offices.

The original 17th-century panelling in this room was removed in the 19th century when the closet was converted into a kitchen. The room has now been restored to its original appearance by the introduction of new panelling, which has been left unstained.

The paintings on the west wall include a profile portrait of Queen Anne, signed by Kneller, and the model for use on coinage and medals. To the right is an oval of her husband, Prince George of Denmark (who died at Kensington Palace in 1708), painted by Michael Dahl in about 1690. Above the fireplace is a still life of fruit by an unknown artist in the style of the 17th-century Italian artist Campidoglio.

Queen Mary's Gallery

Queen Mary's Gallery was originally furnished with fine lacquered chairs, tables and cabinets and 154 pieces of Chinese and Japanese porcelain. The key surviving features of the room are the two overmantel mirrors of Vauxhall plate glass, supplied by Gerrit Jensen, with magnificent carved and gilt surrounds by Grinling Gibbons. The oak panelling, with its elaborately carved cornice, the work of Nicholas Alcock and William

Emmett, also dates from Queen Mary's time, so do the windows, shutters and the grey marble chimneypiece at the far end of the room; the more southerly one is a replacement. The room was originally lit by four chandeliers of gilded wood, suspended down the centre of the room; one of these now hangs in the Queen's Drawing Room.

Fireplace and overmantel in the Queen's Gallery. In Queen Mary II's time, the gallery was filled with 154 pieces of oriental porcelain arranged on and under the tables and cabinets and over the doors and chimneypieces.

When the gallery was first built the panelled walls were hung with silk – the colour 'chosen by the Queen' – with white damask curtains adorning the windows. The present curtains are modern. In the 1720s the panelling was painted white under the direction of William Kent, and the paint was not stripped off again until the restoration of 1898-9.

The large mahogany cabinet standing against the north wall was originally made as an organ case for Queen Caroline in *c*1735 but was converted into a cabinet by William Vile in 1763 on the orders of Queen Charlotte. A concealed entrance in the panelling in the north-west corner of the room led to the apartments of the Maids of Honour.

The splendid full-length portrait of Peter the Great, Tsar of Russia, which hangs on the south wall was painted for William III by Sir Godfrey Kneller during the Tsar's visit to London in 1698. The west wall is hung mainly with family portraits including those of William III and Queen Mary by William Wissing, painted in 1685, and a portrait of Anne Hyde, Duchess of York, first wife of James II and mother of Queen Mary, painted by Sir Peter Lely in about 1662.

The Queen's Staircase

William and Mary's monogram above the garden door on the queen's side of the palace

This plainly decorated staircase, designed by Wren, was primarily used by the Queen to give access between the private apartments and gardens. The carpenter was John Hayward and the oak panelling was made under the direction of the King's Master Joiner, Alexander Fort, who was responsible for the panelling and the fitting of sash windows throughout the palace. The windows on the east side of the staircase still have their original sash frames with typically wide glazing bars and small panes of glass.

The staircase leads down to a hall that was once Queen Mary II's garden room. The garden door, facing the foot of the stairs, dates from 1690-1. Outside, William and Mary's monogram can be seen above the doorway, surrounded by swags of fruit and flowers. This was the work of Thomas Hill, a Master Mason whom Wren had also employed at St Paul's Cathedral.

THE PALACE GARDENS

William III (1689-1702) and Mary II (1689-1694)

In 1664 the gardens of Nottingham House were praised by Samuel Pepys as 'a mighty fine cool place...with a great laver of water in the middle and the bravest place for musique I ever heard'. William and Mary were very keen gardeners so it was perhaps the beauty of the garden which led them to purchase the house and estate in 1689.

William and Mary soon set about extending and improving the gardens, and during the period 1689-96 over £20,000 was spent on them, though this was only a quarter of the expenditure at Hampton Court.

Henry Wise *by Sir Godfrey Kneller, c1715 (detail). Henry Wise was appointed Royal Gardener by Queen Anne in 1702 and for the next 25 years played a leading role in the development of the royal park and gardens at Kensington.*

RIGHT:
Water-colour of a 17th-century tulip, Tulipa suaveolens Roth, *by Herman Henstenburgh. The tulip was very popular during the reign of William and Mary and the Queen's collection of ceramics included several curious pagoda-shaped 'tulip vases' in which these flowers were displayed.*

The south garden of 12 acres was laid out by George London between 1689 and 1691 (*see* illustration, page 7). It was a sophisticated composition of parterre and wilderness arranged either side of a central walk (Dial Walk), and may have been designed by Daniel Marot, a Huguenot who worked for William and Mary in the Netherlands and who designed some of the gardens at Hampton Court.

To the west of the palace a kitchen garden was established, where fruit and vegetables were grown. This was under the supervision of William Kirke, who had a staff of 20. A further 40 men and 10 women were employed maintaining the palace gardens.

The Centifolia Rose, *by Pierre-Joseph Redouté (1759-1840). This flower was much admired in the time of William and Mary.*

In 1701 attention turned to the area to the north of the palace where Henry Wise (in partnership with George London) planted out a formal 'wilderness'. However, work came to an abrupt halt with the death of the King in March 1702.

LEFT:
The Sunken Garden, laid out in 1908-9. The three fountains date from the 18th century and were made from cisterns from the palace.

Queen Anne (1702-1714)

Queen Anne shared with her brother-in-law, William III, whom she otherwise detested, a love of gardening, and during the opening years of her reign £26,000 was spent on improving the estate. One of her first decisions, in the summer of 1702, was to restart the work on the wilderness.

Detail of a plan of Kensington Gardens, c1715, showing the wilderness to the north of the palace, laid out between 1701 and 1704 for William III and Queen Anne.

Henry Wise's planting list for Kensington Gardens 1711-12.

This development of the northern part of the estate more than doubled the size of the gardens and was comprised of areas of thickly planted trees and shrubs, crossed by intersecting walks. Wise shaped a former gravel pit into a series of concentric terraces with topiary and, nearby, planted a block of trees, rising in height towards the centre, thereby simulating a mount. In 1704-5, the Orangery was erected near the entrance to the wilderness (*see* page 39).

The south garden was embellished during Queen Anne's reign with fountains and an alcove at the south end of Dial Walk. Some early engravings of this garden show a modified design of the garden as a whole; these can only represent a proposal as the 1689 layout in fact survived until about 1727.

The alcove was an elaborate Portland stone seat, or summer house, for which payment was made in 1706-7. This grand structure, with Corinthian columns flanking niches on either side of a central alcove, is now located at the north end of the Serpentine, near Lancaster Gate.

A further extension was made to the palace gardens in 1705, when 100 acres of Hyde Park to the east of the palace were acquired to form a paddock for the royal deer and antelope.

George I (1714-1727)

On 1 October 1714 George I paid a visit to Kensington to inspect the gardens and lodgings 'both which he lik't very well'. Throughout his reign the gardens were well managed and well maintained by Henry Wise and it was not until the last years of his life that George ordered any major alterations. In 1725-6 the King introduced a number of exotic animals into the paddock, to the east of the palace, including three tigers and two civet cats. This was accompanied by a decision to enlarge the paddock, roughly doubling its size. Work commenced in 1726 under the direction of the Master Gardener, Charles Bridgeman (until 1728 in partnership with Henry Wise).

George II (1727-1760)

George II's wife, Queen Caroline, was a keen gardener and she saw the paddock as an opportunity for a grand scheme east of the palace. By the end of 1727 George I's tigers and civet cats had been moved to the menagerie at the Tower of London and Caroline enthusiastically pushed forward her ideas, which remain the basis of the present Kensington Gardens. The Broad Walk was formed running north-south alongside the old gardens and wilderness. East of it, a large octagonal basin (the Round Pond) completed in 1728, occupied the centre of a semicircular lawn edged by trees, from which a series of wide tree-lined avenues radiated far into the distance. Some of the areas enclosed by these avenues were planted with young trees and bushes, and some were left as bare lawns. A series of ponds to the east of this layout were flooded to form the Serpentine, and beyond this a terrace with bastions was constructed to form the division from Hyde Park. The work was finished by 1731 and two yachts were placed on the Serpentine 'for the diversion of the Royal Family'.

The new gardens included an earth mount with a spiral path winding its way to the top. This was surmounted by a revolving summer house, designed by William Kent in 1734, from where the King and Queen could survey the whole garden layout. Another summer house nearby, known as

This drawing by Bernard Lens, dated 1736, shows the mount and summer house erected for George II and Queen Caroline near the south-east corner of the gardens. The king's road, which ran from the palace to Hyde Park, can be seen in the foreground with its row of lamps.

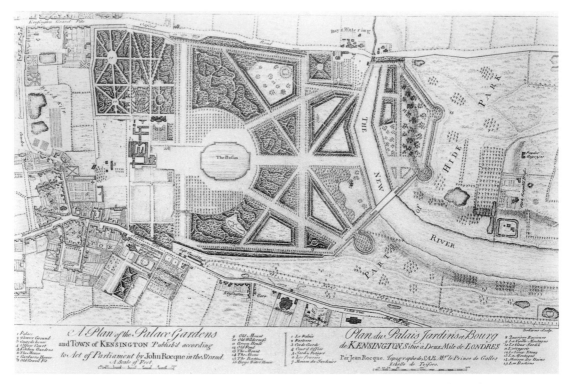

A Plan of the Palace Gardens and Town of Kensington *by John Rocque, 1736. This bird's-eye view shows the gardens during the reign of George II and Queen Caroline. To the north of the palace, Queen Anne's wilderness still survives; to the east are the newly-created Round Pond, Serpentine and the radiating avenues connecting them; to the south, William and Mary's elaborate garden has been swept away and replaced by lawn.*

Queen Caroline *by Joseph Highmore, c1735. The Queen was a very keen gardener and the gardens at Kensington were transformed during this period, under her direction.*

the Queen's Temple, was built in 1734-5 to Kent's design and was framed by an early example of naturalistic planting. This building still survives.

The south garden was also transformed during this period. Tastes in gardening had changed to grand simplicity since it was laid out in the late 17th century and the elaborate design of 1689 was very expensive to maintain. Queen Caroline ordered that the ornate wilderness should be swept away and the whole area laid down to a plain parterre of grass and gravel.

The gardens were opened to the public in George II's reign, but only on Saturdays, when the court moved out to Richmond. In the later 18th century, after Kensington had ceased to be used by the reigning monarch, the gardens and park were open every day and became 'a fashionable promenade during the summer months'.

After 1760 the kitchen gardens became the most important part of the estate at Kensington, being used to supply the royal palaces with fruit and vegetables, wherever the sovereign happened to be in residence. In 1813 the Prince Regent (the future King George IV) ordered a great expansion of these gardens, which almost doubled the area and included new hothouses for growing peaches and pineapples. However, by 1841 the cost of keeping up the gardens had become too great and it was decided to consolidate the royal kitchen gardens at Frogmore. The Kensington kitchen gardens were consequently closed down and the area was later developed with large detached houses, as Kensington Palace Gardens.

40

The Orangery

The Orangery, built in 1704-5, still retains its original terrace of Portland stone. The two brick gate piers to the west, surmounted by large stone vases, marked the northern extent of the gardens before the wilderness was laid out in the early 18th century.

The Orangery (known as the 'Greenhouse' in the late 18th and early 19th centuries), was built for Queen Anne in 1704-5 and was used during the winter months for housing plants, and in the summer for court entertainments. In 1718, for example, The *Post Boy* reported: 'Yesterday

being the Anniversary of HM's Birth Day, the Court at Kensington was more numerous than hath been known for many Years: at night there was a Ball in the Green House.'

The design of the Orangery, attributed to Nicholas Hawksmoor, was modified by Sir John Vanbrugh and the initial estimate of £2,599 had more than doubled by the time work was completed. The building was restored in the late 19th century when much of the panelling was replaced. The panelling, cornice and the 24 Corinthian columns are all painted white, following the original scheme.

The China Orange *by an unknown artist. In 1785 the Orangery at Kensington was fitted with two engines to lift the orange trees that were kept there during the winter months; in the summer they were transferred to the terrace outside.*

Above the arches at either end of the room are pine and pearwood carvings by Grinling Gibbons. Beneath them are niches which now contain four statues of female deities by Pietro Francavilla, bought by Frederick, Prince of Wales in 1751. In the two circular rooms beyond are a pair of large vases sculpted by Caius Gabriel Cibber and Edward Pearce at the end of the 17th century for the gardens at Hampton Court. The surrounding niches contain copies of Roman busts.

The Sunken Garden

LEFT:
The Galande Peach *by William Hooker, 1818. The kitchen gardens at Kensington supplied the sovereign's table with a great variety of fruit and vegetables including peaches, pineapples, cherries, melons, apricots, peas, asparagus and mushrooms.*

The Sunken Garden was laid out during the reign of Edward VII and opened in May 1909 on ground formerly occupied by forcing-houses and potting sheds. It was intended to demonstrate the formal type of garden that had existed at Kensington before it was landscaped in the 18th century, and was modelled on the 'Tudor Garden' at Hampton Court. The three lead fountains were formerly cisterns in the palace.

WILLIAM III
OF ORANGE
KING OF GREAT BRITAIN
AND IRELAND 1689-1702
PRESENTED BY WILLIAM II
GERMAN EMPEROR AND
KING OF PRUSSIA TO
KING EDWARD VII FOR
THE BRITISH NATION
1907

EXTERIOR

The South Front

Architectural detail from the South Front.

The South Front dates from 1695 and was the last addition to Kensington Palace in the reign of William III. Internally, this block provided the King with additional accommodation, while the exterior, aligned on the principle axis of the gardens, became the main architectural feature of the palace.

LEFT:
Bronze statue of William III by Heinrich Baucke outside the South Front of the palace. The statue was presented to King Edward VII in 1907.

ABOVE RIGHT:
A distant view of the South Front from Kensington Gardens.

The façade is topped by four vases carved in Portland stone by Caius Gabriel Cibber. Visible just behind, is William III's wind-vane, which operates the dial in the King's Gallery. In the foreground is a bronze statue of William III by the German sculptor Heinrich Baucke, which was presented to Edward VII by his nephew, Kaiser Wilhelm II in 1907. The range to the west formerly contained the Stone Gallery, and was the residence of the Duke of Sussex (son of George III) from 1805 to 1843. At the end of the path, set into the wall, is an ornamental alcove which formed a feature of the formal gardens laid out at the beginning of the 18th century.

The East Front

The East Front of Kensington Palace with the statue of Queen Victoria, by her daughter Princess Louise, in the foreground.

The large statue of Queen Victoria, beside the Broad Walk, was sculpted by her fourth daughter Princess Louise and shows the Queen at the time of her accession. It was commissioned by the residents of Kensington to commemorate her Golden Jubilee in 1887 and erected in its present location in 1893, in a ceremony attended by the Queen herself. Beyond is the East Front of the palace; the tall block with a round-headed central window and a pediment above highlights the eastern end of the three state rooms rebuilt in 1718-21. Inside is the King's Drawing Room, centrally aligned on the principal features of Kensington Gardens: the Round Pond and the three tree-lined avenues laid out by Charles Bridgeman in the late 1720s.

THE ROYAL CEREMONIAL DRESS COLLECTION

The Royal Ceremonial Dress Collection at Kensington Palace comprises dress worn by members of the Royal Family; dress worn by officials and dignitaries undertaking ceremonial roles, such as heralds or members of Orders of Knighthood; and court dress. The collection dates from the 18th to the late 20th century and is displayed according to several key themes. For conservation reasons the items of dress on show are changed periodically.

A lady in 18th-century court dress from Heideloff's Gallery of Fashion, 1796. *Note the elaborate ostrich feather headdress. This was worn with lace lappets or streamers which were pinned into the hair.*

Court dress was worn by those attending the more formal assemblies and gatherings held by the king or queen. These events were a very important part of the social calendar, and for many years attendance at them was vital for politicians as well as socialites.

Her Majesty's Drawing Room at Buckingham Palace - waiting to be presented, by Arthur Hopkins, 1891.

From the 18th to the 20th century, the most significant event for ladies was known as the 'Drawing Room'. At this ceremony a young girl just out of the schoolroom was presented to the king and queen by a female relation who had previously been presented. This came to mark, symbolically, her entrance into the adult world. In 1902, King Edward VII changed the time of this event to the evening. It was generally held at Buckingham Palace. Gentlemen were presented at a ceremony called a Levée, which took place at St James's Palace.

When meeting the monarch, ladies and gentlemen have always worn the best clothes they could afford. During the early 18th century the mantua and petticoat came to be the accepted wear for ladies at court. This was a fashionable style of the late 17th century and comprised a petticoat worn over side hoops and a bodice with train. At the 18th-century court, the hoops developed to extraordinary size, and remained exclusively a court style of dress long after the fashions moved on.

LEFT:
Detail of Full Dress Civil Uniform, First Class, c1905.

Embroidery detail from a court mantua, c1780.

This style of dress with its wide skirts and train, provided a wonderful opportunity to show off fine silks and elaborate embroidery. One lady went to such extraordinary lengths in 1738 that the commentator Mrs Delany declared 'the pattern much properer for a stucco staircase than the apparel of a lady'.

Gentlemen attending the 18th-century court would wear a suit comprising a coat, waistcoat and knee breeches, made out of the finest fashionable silks, often in vivid colours, and covered with embroidery. Their shoe buckles and sword belts were often decorated with jewels, cut steel or glass paste.

On his accession in 1820, King George IV announced that ladies were no longer required to wear the cumbersome court hoop. However, the train, ostrich feather headdress and lace lappets, or a veil, remained distinctive components of court dress until as late as 1939. George IV also promoted styles of court uniform to replace the colourful court suits worn by 18th-century gentlemen. These uniforms, made of fine wool, were elaborately embroidered with gold and silver wire. The colour of the cloth and the style and position of the embroidery were used to distinguish the office and rank of the wearer. Each uniform reflected military styles of the period in which it was introduced. However, as with the ladies' dress, the styles immediately fossilised and remained unchanged years after the fashion had moved on. Even though court uniform is rarely seen today, many of the styles still have their origins in the early 19th century.

While British court tradition successfully weathered the turbulent years of the First World War, the 1920s saw changes in ladies' court dress. The elaborate trains were reduced in length and skirts became fashionably short. The last occasion ladies had to dress up in this splendid attire was in 1939. After the Second World War court occasions changed their character and this distinctive style of dress was no longer worn.

To service the court, tailors and dressmakers in London and many other fashionable centres specialised in the production of these distinctive clothes. A tailor, based in Savile Row or the City, would have to be aware of all the details of gentlemen's court uniform, as the styles became ever more complex and numerous. From the end of the 19th century, the Lord Chamberlain periodically issued a set of dress regulations to explain what should be worn by each official of every office and rank.

For dressmakers this work also proved important and profitable. However, as the court business was concentrated into a very short

The collection of dresses lent by Her Majesty The Queen includes gowns designed by Sir Norman Hartnell, Sir Hardy Amies and Ian Thomas.

season each year, the seamstresses often had to work very long hours, in poor conditions and for little pay. During the 19th century there were two major Government enquiries which looked into their working conditions and endeavoured to improve them.

The 20th century saw the rise of the couturier. All would compete for commissions as the spectacular court events proved an excellent opportunity to show off the quality of their dress design. Many an aspiring young couturier, such as Norman Hartnell, made his reputation by securing an important client, who would wear one of his distinctive embroidered and beaded court dresses at Buckingham Palace. Very soon many other important customers were flocking to his showroom in Bruton Street, London.

The tailors who supplied court dress were also called upon to make up dress for other kinds of ceremonies. Many great occasions of state, such as coronations or state funerals, have particular costume and textile requirements. The tailor would be well versed in such detail. For example, the small black spots applied to the white fur capes (imitating ermine) on the coronation robes worn by members of the nobility would be very carefully counted and positioned, as this device indicates the seniority of the wearer.

Detail of the coronation robe worn by Queen Mary in 1911.

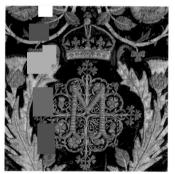

Other items of dress have been preserved by the Royal Family because they are associated with significant moments in the life of the wearer. The most impressive items are the coronation robes, each a skilful blend of splendid decoration, formality, fossilisation and fashion. Dress worn by royal brides reflects to a much greater degree the fashions of the period. Royal ladies have used such opportunities to promote the best of British craft, whether it be in the production of special textiles, fine lace or commissioning designs from a leading couturier or even aspiring student at art school.

Dress worn on less formal occasions has survived because the skills which went into its manufacture were particularly admired. Each monarch has had favourite designers who would produce dress to suit their taste, and which was practical and suitable for the occasion. Dresses worn in Australia might be embroidered with wattle (a native plant) for instance, or California poppies for the United States of America. Bright colours might be used so that the wearer could be easily seen. Nothing was too short or long.

RIGHT:
Dress design by Ian Thomas for Her Majesty The Queen, 1979. Ian Thomas trained with Sir Norman Hartnell and became one of Her Majesty's favourite couturiers.

OPPOSITE:
Court Dress, 1911, worn by Miss Dorothy Polson.

Royal dress provides both tangible evidence of the splendour of court events and, at the same time, truly personal mementos of its wearers. The collection at Kensington Palace is added to with each generation and remains a unique display and archive of British royal fashion.

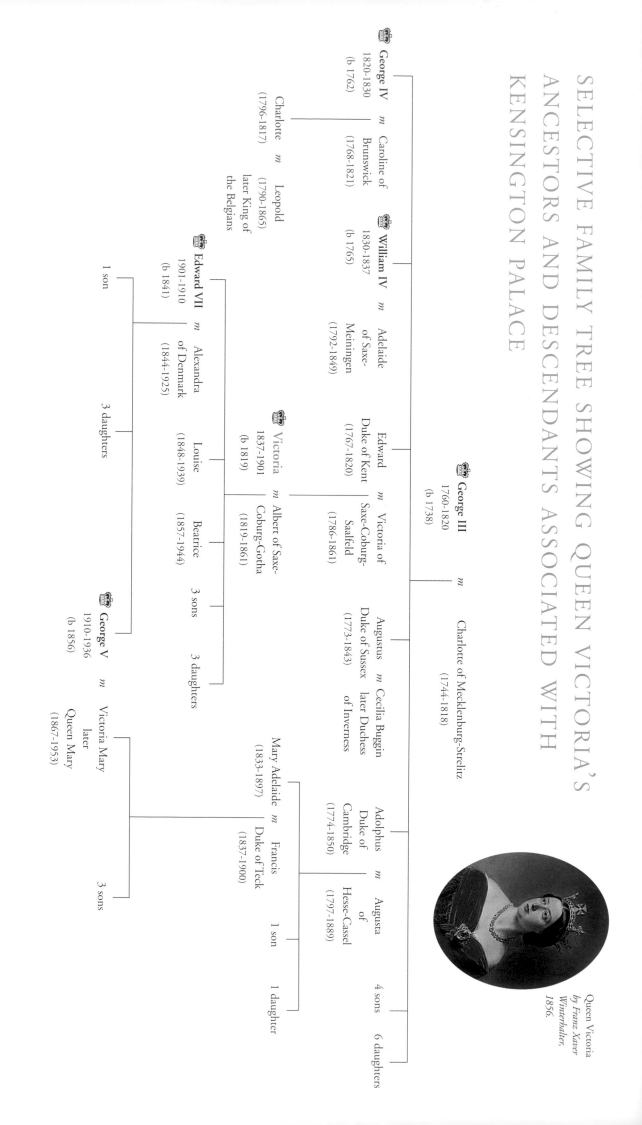

SELECTIVE FAMILY TREE SHOWING QUEEN VICTORIA'S ANCESTORS AND DESCENDANTS ASSOCIATED WITH KENSINGTON PALACE

George III
1760-1820
(b 1738)

m

Charlotte of Mecklenburg-Strelitz
(1744-1818)

George IV
1820-1830
(b 1762)

m

Caroline of
Brunswick
(1768-1821)

William IV
1830-1837
(b 1765)

m

Adelaide
of Saxe-
Meiningen
(1792-1849)

Edward
Duke of Kent
(1767-1820)

m

Victoria of
Saxe-Coburg-
Saalfeld
(1786-1861)

Augustus
Duke of Sussex
later Duke
of Inverness
(1773-1843)

m

Cecilia Buggin
later Duchess
of Inverness

Adolphus
Duke of
Cambridge
(1774-1850)

m

Augusta
of
Hesse-Cassel
(1797-1889)

Charlotte
(1796-1817)

m

Leopold
(1790-1865)
later King of
the Belgians

Victoria
1837-1901
(b 1819)

m

Albert of Saxe-
Coburg-Gotha
(1819-1861)

Mary Adelaide
(1833-1897)

m

Francis
Duke of Teck
(1837-1900)

4 sons

6 daughters

Edward VII
1901-1910
(b 1841)

m

Alexandra
of Denmark
(1844-1925)

Louise
(1848-1939)

Beatrice
(1857-1944)

3 sons

3 daughters

1 son

1 daughter

1 son

3 daughters

George V
1910-1936
(b 1856)

m

Victoria Mary
later
Queen Mary
(1867-1953)

3 sons

*Queen Victoria
by Franz Xaver
Winterhalter,
1856.*

GLOSSARY

Arabesque: A type of curvilinear decoration with intricate intertwining designs.

Couturier: A person who designs, makes and sells high fashion clothes.

Entablature: The whole assemblage of horizontal parts above a column. The three primary divisions are the architrave, cornice and frieze.

Grisaille: A technique of monochrome painting in shades of grey.

Grotesque: A decorative style consisting of scrollwork, foliage, architectural elements, fanciful human figures and fantastic beasts.

Ionic: The second of the Greek orders, of which the main feature is the voluted or scrolled capital (the head or crowning feature of a column or pilaster).

Japanned: Decorated and varnished in the Japanese manner with a glossy durable paint in imitation of black lacquer.

Parterre: A formal garden composed of beds and gravel paths arranged in ornamental patterns.

Trompe l'oeil: A painting, etc, giving a convincing illusion of reality.

ACKNOWLEDGMENTS

Crown copyright © 1998. Published by Historic Royal Palaces, 1998.

Based on an original text by John Haynes. Revised and edited by Clare Murphy. Royal Ceremonial Dress Collection text by Joanna Marschner. Additional material supplied by the Curatorial Department, Historic Royal Palaces.

All research, design and conservation work for the Royal Ceremonial Dress Collection has been undertaken by the Curatorial Department and Textile Conservation Studio, Historic Royal Palaces.

Historic Royal Palaces would also like to thank the following individuals and organisations for their contributions to the redisplay of the Royal Ceremonial Dress Collection: Her Majesty The Queen; The Bowden Collection; Cartier Collection Ancienne; Geneva; Crowns & Regalia Ltd; Ede and Ravenscroft Ltd, London; The Museum of London; Manchester City Art Galleries; the National Portrait Gallery, London; Stockman London Limited and other private lenders and donors. Audioguide organ clock music: *Gigue* by Handel from a clock by George Pyke, c1750. By kind permission of the National Museum of Musical Clocks to Street Organs, Utrecht, Netherlands.

Designed by Schneider Associates Limited. Origination by Essex Colour Limited. Printed by The White Dove Press Limited.

Illustrations

Abbreviations: b = bottom, c = centre, l = left, r = right, t = top.

Unless otherwise stated, all photographs are Crown copyright: Historic Royal Palaces. Photography by Paul Highnam: pages 18, 29r, 30, 31, 33, 34t, 35c, 41t, 46t, 46b, 47, 48t, 49 and front cover. Plans inside front cover and page 8 by Precision Illustration.

The British Library: page 38t (Add MS 42572C). The Trustees of the British Museum: page 3 (Crace Views ix 22-23), 37b. Hulton Getty: page 45b. The Illustrated London News Picture Library: page 15b. Mary Evans Picture Library: page 16t, 45t. The Museum of London: pages 16b, 17, 46tr. The National Portrait Gallery, London: pages 5b, 7b, 9c, 10b, 11c, 14t, 34c. The Pepys Library, Magdalene College, Cambridge: page 6br. Crown copyright material in the Public Record Office is reproduced by permission of the Controller of Her Majesty's Stationery Office: pages 6t (Work 6/5 p143), 38b (Work 5/146). The Royal Archives © 1998 Her Majesty The Queen: pages 14c, 14b. The Royal Botanic Gardens, Kew/Bridgeman Art Library, London: page 40b. The Royal Collection © 1998: Her Majesty The Queen: contents page b, 4, 5t, 9t, 10t, 11t, 12, 13t, 13br, 15t, 19b, 21b, 22b, 23, 26c, 27t, 28c, 29t, 32, 35t, 37t, 40c, 50. The Royal Borough of Kensington & Chelsea Libraries and Arts Service: pages 7t, 11b, 13bl, 26b, 39b, 40t. The Royal Horticultural Society, Lindley Library: page 41l. Teyler Museum, Haarlem: page 37c. The Trustees of the Victoria and Albert Museum: page 39t.

OTHER HISTORIC ROYAL PALACES TO VISIT

The Tower of London
Britain's foremost historical attraction

Work on the Tower was begun by William the Conqueror in the 11th century. Since then it has been a royal palace and fortress, prison, arsenal and treasury. With the Crown Jewels, the Yeoman Warders and the Royal Armouries, it remains Britain's most absorbing historical landmark. Enquiries telephone 0171 709 0765.

Hampton Court Palace
Royal history by the Thames

Five hundred years of royal history are brought to life at Hampton Court, from the preparation of a banquet in Henry VIII's Tudor Kitchens to the magnificence of William III's State Apartments. The palace is set in 60 acres of stunning gardens which include popular features such as the Maze and the Great Vine. Enquiries telephone 0181 781 9500.

The Banqueting House, Whitehall
The original setting for royal banquets

The Banqueting House, with its magnificent Rubens ceiling, was designed by the renowned architect Inigo Jones in the early 17th century and is today the only remaining part of Whitehall Palace. Charles I, the only English monarch to be executed, met his fate here. Enquiries telephone 0171 930 4179.

Kew Palace
The royal home in the gardens

Dating from 1631, this is one of the smaller royal palaces and is set in the Royal Botanic Gardens. It provides an intriguing glimpse of royal domestic life in the early part of the 19th century. **Closed for refurbishment until Spring 2001.**

Queen Charlotte's Cottage
The royal summer house in the gardens

The cottage, also in the Royal Botanic Gardens at Kew, was built in 1772 and named after Queen Charlotte, consort to George III. The royal family used it as a summer house and often took tea there.

More information on the Historic Royal Palaces is available on the official web site: http://www.hrp.org.uk

LONDON™